Tornado!

BY ELIZABETH RAUM

AMICUS HIGH INTEREST • AMICUS INK

Amicus High Interest and Amicus Ink are imprints of Amicus
P.O. Box 1329, Mankato, MN 56002
www.amicuspublishing.us

Library of Congress Cataloging-in-Publication Data
Names: Raum, Elizabeth, author.
Title: Tornado! / by Elizabeth Raum.
Description: Mankato, MN : Amicus, [2017] | Series: Natural
  disasters | Audience: K to Grade 3. | Includes index.
Identifiers: LCCN 2015031586 (print) | LCCN 2016002857
  (ebook) | ISBN 9781607539926 (library binding) | ISBN
  9781607539988 (ebook) | ISBN 9781681520858 (pbk.)
  | ISBN 9781607539988 (pdf)
Subjects: LCSH: Tornadoes–Juvenile literature.
Classification: LCC QC955.2 .R382 2017 (print) | LCC
  QC955.2 (ebook) | DDC 551.55/3–dc23
LC record available at http://lccn.loc.gov/2015031586

Editor: Wendy Dieker
Series Designer: Kathleen Petelinsek
Book Designer: Tracy Myers
Photo Researcher: Rebecca Bernin

Photo Credits: Willoughby Owen/Getty cover; Minerva Studio/
Shutterstock 5; Martin Haas/Shutterstock 6; antonyspencer/
iStock 8-9; Associated Press 10; Minerva Studio/Shutterstock
13; AFP/Stringer/Getty 14; eyecrave/iStock 17; NASA/
Corbis 18; Associated Press 20-21; Associated Press 22; Jim
Reed/Corbis 25; Associated Press 26; Cultura Science/Jason
Persoff Stormdoctor/Getty 29

Printed in the United States of America.

HC 10 9 8 7 6 5 4 3 2 1
PB 10 9 8 7 6 5 4 3 2 1

Table of Contents

Wailing Sirens

It's a hot day in May. The sky looks green. The tornado siren wails. You and your family head to the basement and turn on the radio. The weather reporter says a tornado has been spotted 3 miles (4.8 km) north of town. You wait. You listen for the roar of winds. Suddenly, the siren stops. The tornado missed you. You are safe.

A tornado is a spinning column of wind that reaches from the clouds down to the ground.

A tornado is like a giant vacuum cleaner. It can pick up cars and tear roofs off houses.

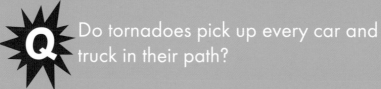 Do tornadoes pick up every car and truck in their path?

A tornado is a giant tower of air. It is also called a twister. Twisters rip roofs off houses and tear down barns. They lift trucks off the ground and drop them miles away. They suck up almost everything in their path. They twist and turn. Sometimes they strike one building but miss the next.

 No. Scientists don't know why twisters lift some and not others.

Most tornadoes occur in the spring and early summer. During the day, the sun heats the ground. The heat rises. A thunderstorm brings cool, wet air. The warm, dry air meets the cool, wet air. It can make the storm clouds spin. They spin faster and faster. The spinning air pulls the cloud down into a funnel shape. It becomes a tornado!

Storm clouds form over warm ground. Will they start to spin?

8

Dr. Ted Fujita studies a tornado machine. He learns about how air moves in these storms.

Q How fast are the winds in an EF5 tornado?

How Bad Is It?

Dr. Ted Fujita wanted a way to describe tornado damage. He came up with the **Fujita Scale**. In 2007, it was updated. It is now called the Enhanced Fujita (EF) Scale. Most twisters are weak. They break branches off trees. They bend signs. These are called EF0. The worst storms are EF5. They carry away houses. They throw cars into the air.

 No one knows for sure. They probably blow over 200 **mph** (322 **kph**).

About seven out of ten tornadoes are EF0 or EF1. They do little harm. Many happen in open areas. About two in ten are EF2 or EF3. They tear roofs off houses. They blow down trees. They can even strip the bark off trees. Only one in ten is an EF4 or EF5. They are killers.

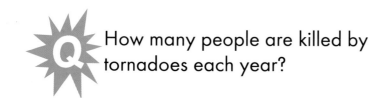

How many people are killed by tornadoes each year?

A twister in an open area throws around dirt and damages crops. Not many people get hurt.

 In 2015, 10 people died in U.S. tornadoes. When tornadoes hit big cities, more people might die.

Terrible Twisters

The United States has more than 1,200 tornadoes a year. That's more than any other place. But these storms can happen in almost any country in the world. The worst ever was in Bangladesh in Asia. In 1989, a tornado killed 1,300 people. More than 12,000 people were hurt. About 80,000 people lost their homes. It took years to rebuild.

A man in Bangladesh helps clean up after the 1989 tornado destroyed his village.

On May 22, 2011, an EF5 tornado hit the crowded city of Joplin, Missouri. It killed 158 people. More than 1,000 people were hurt. The tornado blew down houses and schools. Stores and offices were destroyed. The twister was on the ground for 22 miles (35.4 km). It was 1 mile (1.6 km) wide. It lasted 38 minutes. Then it died away.

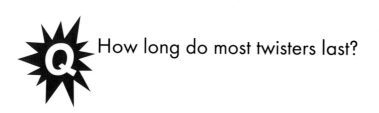 How long do most twisters last?

People in Joplin, Missouri, dug through flattened homes after the 2011 tornado.

 Most last about eight minutes. Stronger ones last longer.

This image from space shows
many tornadoes forming over
the southeastern United States.

Q Why were there so many twisters?

Sometimes many tornadoes hit at about the same time. It's called a **cluster**. From April 26 to 28, 2011, over 300 twisters formed in 17 states. Four were EF5s. The state of Alabama was hardest hit. More than 230 people died there. Another 2,200 were hurt. One twister was nearly 1 mile (1.6 km) wide. That's huge!

There were many thunderstorms. Nine out of ten became twisters. That's rare. No one knows why it happened.

Hail often falls before a tornado touches down. On June 16, 2014, hail as big as ping-pong balls fell on Pilger, Nebraska. A twister followed. And then a second twister formed. The two joined together and swept through town. They destroyed the fire station and more than 40 homes. Two people died.

Twin tornados are rare. These two hit Pilger, Nebraska in 2014.

A scientist studies computer images of the weather. Is a tornado going to form?

Q Where do most North Amercian tornadoes strike?

Predicting Storms

Tornadoes are not easy to **predict**.
In the United States, the National
Weather Service (NWS) tracks storms.
Scientists called **meteorologists** study the
weather. They use **radar** to watch what's
happening. Radar shows strong winds
moving in. It shows rain falling. They
check the air temperature. Could a twister
form?

 Tornadoes touch down most often in the
plains between the Rocky Mountains
and Applachian Mountains. This part of
the continent is called Tornado Alley.

After checking the weather, the NWS sends out storm warnings. If the weather is right for a tornado to form, the NWS sends a **tornado watch**.

Sometimes spotters see clouds spinning. Then the NWS sends out a **tornado warning**. The warning goes out over radio and TV stations. Sirens go off. It's time to take cover.

 Should I take pictures of the tornado?

This truck carries tools used to study and predict tornados.

No! These storms are very dangerous. Take cover and stay in a safe place until the storm is over.

Students practice taking cover during a tornado drill. They know what to do in case a tornado hits.

What if I'm at school when a tornado strikes?

Staying Safe

In case of a tornado, everyone should know what to do. If your house has a basement, go there. If not, go to the lowest floor. Stay away from windows. Choose a small central room like a bathroom. Crouch near the floor and cover your head with your hands. Do not stay in a mobile home or a car. You are safer outside.

 Follow the drill! Your teachers know what to do. Stay with your class and go to the safest place in the building.

If you are caught away from home, go to a sturdy building. If you cannot do that, go to an open field. Stay away from trees. Find a ditch or a low spot in the field and crouch down. Wait for the tornado to pass.

Remember, tornadoes blow over quickly. Few people ever see them. Even so, it's smart to be prepared.

Glossary

cluster A group of tornadoes that touch down at about the same time or in about the same area.

Fujita Scale A way to measure tornado damage.

kph An abbreviation for kilometers per hour; this tells how far an object travels in one hour.

meteorologist A scientist who studies weather.

mph An abbreviation for miles per hour; this tells how far an object travels in one hour.

predict To guess what will happen in advance.

radar A tool using radio waves that makes images of solid objects; meteorologists use radar to see where clouds and rain are.

tornado warning A warning issued by the National Weather Service when a tornado is on the ground; people should take cover.

tornado watch A warning issued by the National Weather Service when the weather is such that a tornado could form.

Read More

Fradin, Judith Bloom and Dennis B Fradin. *Tornado!: The Story Behind These Twisting, Turning, Spinning, and Spiraling Storms.* Washington, D.C.: National Geographic, 2011.

Kostigen, Thomas. *Extreme Weather: Surviving Tornadoes, Sandstorms, Hailstorms, Blizzards, Hurricanes, and More!* Washington, D.C.: National Geographic, 2014.

Miller, Ron. *Chasing the Storm: Tornadoes, Meteorology, and Weather Watching.* Minneapolis: Twenty-First Century Books, 2014.

Websites

Kids' Crossing: Tornado Safety
http://www.eo.ucar.edu/kids/dangerwx/tornado5.htm

KIDSTORM: Tornadoes
http://skydiary.com/kids/tornadoes.html

Weather Wiz Kids: Tornadoes
http://www.weatherwizkids.com/weather-tornado.htm

Index

About the Author

Elizabeth Raum has worked as a teacher, librarian, and writer. She says, "Storms are exciting." She has lived through blizzards and floods. She's seen a tornado in the distance. She watched earthquakes, hurricanes, and wildfires on the Weather Channel. It's safer! Visit her website at: www.elizabethraum.net.